Published by: Writers Publishing House

Printed in the United States

Paperback ISBN: 978-1-64873-558-5

eBook ISBN: 978-1-64873-559-2

Through My Own Eyes

Bridget Mitchell

Contents

CHAPTER 1

FIRST LOVE AND DISCOVERY

My memories of that day remain sharp—returning home from school with a heart full of excitement, my thoughts were consumed by a high school crush. For the first time, someone showed me genuine affection, expressed through daily love letters I kept tucked away in a locker to hide from prying eyes. Two days later, my mother found a note in my pocket. The look on her face told me everything without saying a word.

"What is this, and don't lie?" she quipped.

My face turned fire red, but I played dumb. "She just writes me letters, that's all."

"So, is this the same girl who comes over and sits with you all afternoon?"

I laughed nervously. "Yeah, I guess so..."

Her expression said it all. "So, you are gay?"

"What? No, I'm not gay. It's just a girl from school who likes to write me letters."

My explanation didn't matter. She glared at me, stormed off, but came back ten minutes later, fuming. "You will not see her again, and she's not allowed in this house."

I tried to explain, "Well, that's impossible… I'm the manager of the girls' basketball team. I have to see her every day."

"Well, then, you have some decisions. Stop seeing her or leave home."

Heartbroken, I chose the only option I felt I had: sneak around to be with my crush, whom I'll call Hoops.

Eventually, her ultimatum became a reality. My mother met me at the door. "I don't like liars or lesbians in my house. That's nasty and a sin."

In tears, I asked, "Where am I supposed to go?"

"It does not matter. You will not stay here. I warned you."

My sisters cried, "You can't kick her out. What is she supposed to do? She takes care of us when you're not here." They continued to cry. My mother didn't care. She had this mean streak about her.

I walked down the steps, loneliness overtaking me, yet relief came too—finally, the truth was out, well, at least to my family.

The day after being put out, the walk home from school began like every other. My feet traced the same path taken countless times before, yet something in the air felt different. Halfway down the block came the sudden realization—returning wasn't possible. That house no longer felt like home.

Movement stopped. My eyes lingered on the familiar street, memories pressing heavy against my chest. No place remained to go. Tears followed as the truth sank in. A whisper escaped, "I can't go there anymore." Speaking it made everything real.

Crying came easily on that walk toward a friend's house. The moment the door opened, the tears explained enough. No words were needed. A couch offered shelter for the night. Lying there, long after silence filled the room, my thoughts raced through the darkness. Just days earlier, there had been a routine, a family, a sense of belonging. Now, in a different living room, uncertainty waited for morning.

Blankets pulled tighter promised small comfort against the emptiness. Crying again felt wrong—weak, maybe even ungrateful. Gratitude didn't erase the feeling of being lost. That night marked the first true understanding of independence. Still only a teenager, life had forced an early reckoning.

Later, when the truth came out—how the letters had been found and led to me being put out—nervousness filled the moment. Speaking made everything more real. My friend listened, her face caught between shock and sadness. Silence stretched while two teenagers tried to comprehend a situation too large for their years.

Blame tempted me, but deep down, the cause was clear. The letters themselves were not the problem; honesty was. Being truthful about my identity had cost me a home.

Hoops didn't try to make excuses or explain it away. Instead, she just listened. Sometimes that was all I needed—someone to hear me without judgment. In that moment, I realized that even though I lost my home, I hadn't completely lost the one person who made me feel understood.

After staying at a friend's house for a few months, I finally called my biological father. We were not close. I barely knew him, but I had no one else to call. He arranged for me to stay in an apartment in his sister's building—rules included keeping up with upgrades and staying out of trouble. This gave me freedom and a way to see Hoops daily.

Hoops always said, "Don't be afraid of who you are. Own your identity." She didn't announce to the world that she was gay, and she wasn't ashamed of who she was either.

Our dating remained secret because I wasn't ready to come out. I wasn't ready for questions to be answered. People whispered and asked questions, but we laughed it off. We were inseparable. She was a sophomore; I was a freshman. For the three years we were together, Hoops took care of me and made sure I was safe. Drama only fueled our closeness. We practically lived together. She was at my apartment almost every day.

We would stay up late talking about life. Hoops always said, "Don't be afraid of who you are. Own your identity."

I never knew what she meant until later in life. Hoops would protect me from the other players. They would tease me, calling me the water girl, and she knew that upset me, but she would comfort me as always.

It was prom time, and everyone was asking Hoops who could take her. The star on the boys' basketball team was crazy about Hoops.

He had asked her to be his prom date, and we looked at each other and laughed, "Hell naw," and walked off. So I was Hoops' prom date, secretly.

We wanted to dance that night but couldn't because neither of us wanted anyone to know we were a couple. I was okay with that, though, because simply being in her presence felt like everything I had ever wanted. It felt like living in a fairy tale. As the night ended, Hoops took me home.

She stayed for a while, put on some music, and we danced—a perfect gentlewoman.

"I couldn't let this night end without getting my prom dance in with you," she replied.

CHAPTER 2

LEAVING HOME AND FIRST HEARTBREAK

Overnight, life inside that house shifted for good. Hoops' departure for college left a hollow space where laughter and routine once lived. The walls that had sheltered childhood now pressed in, heavy with tension and words that refused to fade.

Silence settled in. For the first time, solitude became constant. No one seemed to grasp the emptiness left behind by a first love that had shaped so much of who I was becoming. Searching for connection became a habit—brief encounters, small sparks of curiosity, attempts to fill what had been lost. Desire, intimacy, and boundaries became lessons learned through trial, discovery, and disappointment. There was even a stretch of time spent dating men, hoping maybe something would fit differently. Nothing did. The heart already knew its truth.

By the close of that chapter, clarity arrived—love wounds deeply, identity demands protection, and no one replaces a first love. Life simply teaches how to keep moving while carrying it.

Graduation day should have felt triumphant. Excitement filled the air, yet the moment carried its own kind of ache. My mother stayed away, silence stretched between us, and my sisters—still too young—couldn't attend. Pride stood beside loneliness that day. Then Hoops' mother appeared, holding a card written in familiar handwriting—a final message of care passed through another. Gratitude came easily; emptiness remained.

CHAPTER 3

LESSONS LEARNED AND MEETING OLD MAN

Life has a way of surprising you. Just when I thought I was set on exploring casual relationships, fate introduced me to someone unexpected.

It happened at a summer barbecue. My sister introduced me to an intriguing man, older than anyone I had dated before. At first, I was skeptical. He knew I preferred women, yet there was something about his presence—steady, patient, commanding attention without trying—that made me listen.

We talked. We laughed. Hours passed without my noticing. Old Man promised care, patience, and respect—something I hadn't felt in a long time. His energy was grounding, yet he sparked a curiosity I didn't know I had left.

At first, I was skeptical. He knew my preferences, yet there was something about him. I've always had my guard up, but I let it down just a little bit. We went out for months, and he didn't like coming into my studio apartment.

So, through him, I moved from my aunt's apartment into a big, beautiful home he helped me secure. Life, for a moment, felt safe. He gave me comfort, stability, and the illusion of security.

But nothing that seems perfect ever truly is. In the quiet moments, I noticed subtle red flags—control, manipulation, the shadow behind charm. Life was about lessons, and Old Man was one of the toughest. He became one of my hardest lessons: not everything that feels safe is safe, and not everything that looks like love actually is. Learning to recognize love's difference from possessiveness, care from control.

CHAPTER 4

LOVE, ABUSE, AND MOTHERHOOD

Life with Old Man started out hopeful and slowly turned into something heavy. What first looked like love and care gradually tightened into control, manipulation, and at times, abuse. The smiles and attention created an illusion of belonging while darkness crept in so slowly it almost went unnoticed.

When Old Man and I first met, he claimed not to have a problem with past relationships with women. Those words felt genuine, as though my history didn't bother him at all. Over time, the truth revealed itself—he didn't like gay people, and that tolerance had only been an act. One day, a phone call shattered the routine. Hoops was in town visiting from college and had somehow found my number. Hearing her voice after years apart stirred memories that felt both distant and familiar. She said, "I would love to see you before I head back to college." After a pause, the answer came: "Okay, sure."

Hours passed on the phone, catching up on old times and sharing where life had taken each of us. Eventually, we agreed to meet for dinner. There was nothing romantic about the plan—just two people who had once been close reconnecting after years. At the restaurant, conversation flowed easily. Laughter circled around the past, high school stories, and the ways life had changed. In many ways, time seemed to fold, yet the old feelings were gone. What remained that night felt like friendship and nostalgia, not a rekindled romance.

Later that night, returning home felt routine until I saw Old Man sitting there. His presence made the room feel instantly heavy. "Where have you been?"

"I was out having dinner with an old friend."

Anger flashed in his eyes before another word was spoken. Then, without explanation, he reached over and pressed play on a recorder. The sound of my voice filled the room—the call with Hoops from earlier that day. The moment she said she was in town and wanted to see me played back like evidence.

He stared hard and asked, "So this is who you want to be with?"

Before there was time to process what was happening, rage exploded. His voice rose, sharp and accusing, insisting there had been secret plans to see women behind his back.

Everything escalated in seconds. The situation turned violent, and suddenly there was a broken nose and a stunned silence. "You can pack your bags and leave if you think you're going to be seeing women behind my back. I don't like gays."

The words echoed with a painful familiarity. The moment pulled me back to the day my mother had put me out, the same rejection for loving who I loved.

Attempts to explain came through a shaking voice—she had just been visiting from college, only wanted to see an old friend. That night, leaving didn't happen. Staying didn't mean everything was okay; staying meant there was nowhere else to go. Somewhere inside that chaos, a different future quietly waited—the future that would bring children, love, and purpose into one of the hardest chapters of life.

When pregnancy entered the story, the first feeling wasn't joy—it was fear. Readiness for motherhood simply wasn't there. Life already felt unstable, identity still forming, and survival itself seemed like a full-time job. The idea of bringing a child into all of that felt overwhelming. The weight of past rejections, instability, and constant survival sat heavy on the chest.

The news came in a doctor's office. Sitting in that sterile room, thoughts spun wildly through everything else going on. Motherhood hadn't even been on the mental list yet. Survival of the current life still felt like more than enough.

When the doctor walked in, the words came out simple: "You're pregnant. Congratulations, Mom."

For a moment, the world went quiet. The mind stalled, trying to process what had just been spoken.

The drive home unfolded in silence. Those words replayed over and over. Uncertain about the future stretched out like a long road with no end. So by the time the front door opened, it was clear the Old Man had to know. Keeping something like that a secret was never an option. His reaction surprised me. His face lit up, genuinely excited by the news, even with several children from other women.

In the months that followed, a softer side emerged. He became more affectionate, supportive, and attentive than ever before. For a while, life almost felt stable. After our son was born, that softness faded. The anger returned. Possessiveness grew. Within that shift, a quiet realization settled in—staying like this forever wasn't an option. Plans to leave began forming in the back of the mind, but every time a step toward the door appeared, another pregnancy followed. The second baby, a daughter, arrived a year and a half later.

Old Man felt thrilled at the news of another child; the same excitement didn't rise in me. The thought of bringing another baby into an abusive environment felt wrong. After our daughter's birth, the violence and emotional damage continued. About a year later, a breaking point arrived. Leaving became the only path toward any kind of future.

Walking away from that house ranked among the hardest decisions ever made. Leaving didn't come from a lack of love for the children. Leaving came from the need to survive, to find firm ground and build strength. There were no resources, no stability, and no practical way to take them along. Stepping out alone meant stepping into a life that looked, from the outside, like freedom—but on the inside, every thought circled back to those kids.

For a while, life drifted—work, days, nights, moments that should have looked like fun but never quite felt like it. An ache followed every move, the ache of separation. Then, one day, an old friend appeared: JB. Years had passed since our paths crossed. We began like any two old friends—

talking, catching up, spending time together with no agenda. For about six months, that's all it was.

Somewhere along the way, friendship shifted into something deeper. Dating came naturally. Being around JB felt easy, familiar, like being seen by someone who knew an earlier version of me. After some time, she asked me to move in. What JB didn't yet know was the full weight of the story being carried. She knew children existed, and that they were living with their father, but the deeper history remained unspoken.

Eventually, the silence became too heavy. The truth came out—the abusive relationship, the reasons for leaving without the children, the constant ache of being away from them. The pain of that separation showed, no matter what we did or where we went. A part of me always lived with those kids in my thoughts. JB listened, but processing that reality wasn't easy. She had never been fond of children, and that fact lingered like a quiet warning in the back of my mind.

When the conversation finally turned to bringing the children to live with us, the look on

JB's face said everything. Shock. Frustration. A sense of having been surprised. She reminded me that kids had never been part of the plan, that the idea of them moving in had never been discussed. The room grew tense as the truth settled between us—life had just taken another sharp, unexpected turn.

Inside, the decision had already been made. Those children needed their mother, and the mother needed them. After everything that had happened, leaving them behind a second time was impossible. In that moment, the choice became obvious: choose the children and face whatever came next together.

When the kids finally came home, they were still so young—full of curiosity, energy, and simple joy at just being near their mother again. Every small moment felt sacred. Hearing their laughter, watching them play, holding them close at night— these everyday moments became priceless. The first week in the house felt quiet, but tense. Everyone was adjusting. JB had never imagined children living there, and suddenly, two little lives filled the space.

Slowly, something shifted. JB noticed the joy that came from being a mother again. She watched the way those kids clung to me, the way we loved each other openly. Little by little, her heart slowly opened. The tension in the house softened as everyone learned how to live together under one roof. Over time, JB moved from simply tolerating the kids to actively helping raise them. They grew to love her as well.

Life looked like a family. Vacations, quiet days at home, and simple routines became part of the rhythm. The children needed structure and guidance, and JB stepped into that role in ways that surprised both of us. She wasn't afraid to set boundaries when needed, and that balance was important. Parenting is rarely easy, and having someone willing to stand in the hard moments made a difference.

During that season, JB offered the support needed while life was being rebuilt piece by piece. Together, we learned what it meant to form a family in our own way. Confidence slowly returned. The person taking shape felt stronger, more grounded. Raising children, creating a home, and receiving genuine support after so much loneliness shifted how life looked and felt. For the first time in a long time, it truly felt like standing on my own two feet.

Thoughts often drifted back to something Hoops used to say: "Own your identity. Don't be afraid of who you are."

Those words stayed close, even when their meaning wasn't yet fully understood. Looking at the life being built—for the children and for myself—it finally became clear that the message had taken root. Acceptance of self was no longer a distant goal. Living in truth, without hiding or apologizing, had become a daily practice.

What began as a friendship with JB turned into a long, complicated chapter. The relationship wasn't perfect, but a life was built together with the tools available. Over the years, there were highs and lows—times of closeness and times of separation—yet somehow, we always circled back into each other's lives. In total, about fifteen years were spent in and out of one another's worlds. During those years, children were raised, a home was shared, vacations were taken, and memories were woven together, just like many other long-term relationships marked by both stability and struggle.

JB stood as independent and confident, a police officer studying law, grounded in her own ambition. Fifteen years of adult love brought hard-won lessons—patience, commitment, partnership, and the reality that love can hold both comfort and challenge at once.

During those years, life expanded. A first home was bought, work as an LPN continued, and nursing studies moved forward. The world felt full—busy, demanding, but meaningful. Then came a phone call that would split life into a "before" and "after."

The call came from a detective. At first, the conversation felt confusing. The detective asked if there was a place to sit or if someone was nearby. Confusion filled the space between words. Just hours earlier, there had been a conversation with my daughter. She had been alive, her voice familiar and bright. Then came the words: there was a need to come to the morgue to identify a body—my daughter's body.

In that instant, reality shattered. The world around felt distant, sounds muffled, movements disconnected from the body. The mind refused to accept the words. It could not be true. She had just been on the phone. She was supposed to be waiting to be picked up after work, like always. A scream tore out from a place deeper than anything ever felt before, loud enough for the entire hospital to hear.

When the detectives insisted on the morgue identification, the meaning was clear. The heart, however, could not bear it. Going there, seeing her like that, was more than the soul could carry. Instead, JB went in my place, and my mother went as well. Years of distance between us didn't matter in that moment. The only thing that mattered was Nicole.

They went to the morgue; staying behind felt like floating in a numb, empty world. The last conversation with Nicole replayed over and over—

her voice, her laugh, the normalcy of that evening before everything changed. That night, life turned in a way no parent is ever prepared for.

When they returned, no one had words. Their eyes, their arms, their quiet presence said everything. They held me while grief tore through every part of my being. The crying that followed felt unlike anything before, as if a piece of the heart had been ripped away. Nothing prepares a parent for losing a child. The world outside kept moving, but time inside seemed to stop. Holding my son became the only instinct that made sense.

In the months that followed Nicole's death, numbness settled in. The body went through the motions while the heart stayed somewhere else. Staying at JB's house for a while felt necessary. Going back home—back to the place where Nicole had lived, laughed, and played—felt impossible.

Nicole carried a spirit all her own. Sweet, funny, and just the right amount of mischievous. Teasing her older brother became a favorite game.

She knew exactly how to push his buttons. Sometimes she would turn to him and say, "You know our mother is gay," and the moment the words left her mouth, he would start crying while she burst into laughter, thinking it was the funniest thing in the world.

Alongside that playful streak lived a gentle, creative side. Nicole could sit for hours with her dolls, flipping through magazines, gently combing their hair like a tiny stylist lost in her own world. She loved her movies and shows, especially "Crooklyn" and "House Party."

She would sit completely absorbed, eyes fixed on the screen, now and then glancing up to say, "Mama, you are so pretty."

Those small daily moments have become the most precious memories. They felt ordinary, but looking back now, they are treasures that will remain in the heart forever.

CHAPTER 5

REBUILDING AND REDISCOVERY

After losing my daughter, life felt like an endless storm. Grief was heavy, suffocating, a shadow that clung to every breath I took. Every corner of my world reminded me of what I had lost. And yet, for my son, I had to keep moving. Life couldn't stop, even when I wanted it to.

The first months were survival—learning to breathe without her in the house, without her laughter echoing in the halls. But slowly, I eventually reclaimed myself. I built routines, minor victories: waking up, making breakfast, keeping the apartment clean, showing up for my son, even when I felt empty inside.

JB stayed close during this time. At first, I didn't know if I wanted anyone near me. How could anyone understand this depth of pain? But she did. Her presence was steady, reliable. We argued sometimes, laughed other times, and in both, I found a strange comfort. She became my anchor, a reminder that life, even after unimaginable loss, could still offer connection.

I threw myself into work. Working in the medical field gave me purpose, a reason to step outside my grief and care for others. Every patient I helped, every life I touched, reminded me that even in darkness, there was light. Studying to advance my career gave me structure and focus. Slowly, I rebuilt confidence, independence, and a sense of accomplishment.

Through it all, I learned resilience. I learned the importance of self-love—not just the easy, feel-good kind, but the gritty, determined kind that keeps you standing when the world feels against you. I learned that rebuilding isn't about erasing the past; it's about creating space for new moments, new joys, new love.

JB became more than a friend. She became a partner in the truest sense—someone who accepted my children, my past, and my scars. Our connection was neither perfect nor effortless, but it was real. And in reality, real is everything.

By the end of this chapter of life, I realized something vital: you can endure pain without losing yourself. You can be broken and still choose to build. You can be afraid and still take steps forward. Rebuilding wasn't just about life after tragedy—it was about finding me again, piece by piece, day by day, heartbeat by heartbeat.

And out of nowhere, guess who returned in my life? Hoops came back into the picture.

At that point in my life, I had grown in ways I didn't even realize until I was face-to-face with my past again. We reconnected and spent months together, trying to see if there was still something there, something worth holding on to. I think part of me wanted to believe the chemistry we once had still existed; maybe it was time that hadn't changed everything between us. But as time went on, I saw it for what it was. It didn't feel the same.

What once felt natural now felt like we were trying too hard to bring back something that had already run its course. The realization was difficult because it meant accepting that just because someone was once a big part of your life doesn't mean they'll be there forever. Some things are meant to be experienced, not recreated. That moment gave me defined clarity. It showed me how much I had grown and how important it was to keep moving forward even when the past tries to revisit.

CHAPTER 6

BECOMING A POLICE OFFICER

After years of heartbreak, loss, and rebuilding, I knew I needed a new challenge—a purpose that demanded everything I had, body and soul. Becoming a police officer.

When I got the letter saying I had been accepted, I felt excited. It was a surprise. What started out as something I did just for kicks and giggles suddenly became an opportunity.

At the time, I was working as an LPN and in nursing school, working toward a completely unique path. When the letter came, I started thinking about what this new direction could mean for my life. I told myself that nursing school could always be there. I figured if things didn't work out, I could always go back and finish.

Unfortunately, life had other plans, and I never returned to nursing school. But at that moment, standing at the crossroads, I took a chance on something new. It was a decision that would change the course of my life in ways I never could have imagined.

When I first walked into the police academy, nerves took over. The whole place felt like a different world, and part of me questioned whether the decision had been the right one. Luckily, JB was there to guide me through it, and she understood exactly what the academy would demand.

It wasn't easy. The physical training, the discipline, and the constant pressure pushed me harder than anything I had faced before. Some days felt close to impossible, and quitting crossed my mind more than once.

Knowing everyone who worked at the academy before I started made things even more interesting. Some people might have expected special treatment, but it was the opposite. No favors were given, and if anything, the expectations were even higher. Still, there was support behind it all. Those same people wanted to see me succeed, and that encouragement made a difference on the days when everything felt like too much.

The day I graduated from the police academy was one of the greatest achievements of my life. After all the hard days, the training, and the moments when I wanted to give up, I finally reached the finish line. Standing there, looking out into the crowd, I saw familiar faces that meant the world to me. My son was there, along with JB and a few close friends. Their support had carried me through the journey, and seeing them in that moment reminded me how far I had come.

But there was one person I never expected to see: my mother. Seeing her brought tears to my eyes. So much had happened between us over the years, and there were long stretches when we barely spoke. I never imagined she'd be standing there that day.

After the ceremony, when she looked at me and said, "I'm so proud of you," I was shocked. Those were words I never thought I would hear from her. Something inside me healed just a little.

All the struggle, pain, and long road that led me there suddenly felt worth it.

That day, I didn't just graduate from the academy. I stepped into a new chapter of my life.

Patrol differed from anything I'd experienced. It showed me the full range of humanity—the beauty, the tragedy, and the chaos. With every call and every street I walked, I learned lessons that went far beyond textbooks or classrooms.

Two moments stayed with me in particular. The first was simple but powerful. Two little girls were playing in a park on my beat. One of them walked over and asked, "Officer, can you stay here for a while so my sister and I can play?"

I parked the squad car and stayed with them for the rest of my tour. Watching them laugh and seeing the joy on their faces reminded me of why I chose this path. Small moments like that— moments of safety, trust, and connection—were the real victories of the job.

The second was painfully familiar. I received a call about a shooting involving a young man I had known. Standing with the detectives as they informed his mother that her son was gone, I felt a grief so raw it clawed through me. It brought back memories of my daughter. My chest ached, my throat burned, but it also reminded me why my work mattered. I could use my position to prevent other families from facing the same unimaginable pain.

By this time, it wasn't just about enforcing the law—it was about empathy, courage, and resilience. Every shift tested me in ways I never expected. I met people at their worst, saw the consequences of choices and chance, and witnessed moments of pure human connection.

Through all of it, I discovered new strengths in myself. I learned that courage isn't just physical—it's emotional. It's standing up for someone who can't, listening when no one else will, and carrying the weight of human suffering without losing your own humanity.

My journey as an officer didn't erase my past. It didn't heal all wounds. But it gave me purpose. It gave me focus. And it reminded me every single day that life—no matter how brutal or beautiful—was worth being present.

CHAPTER 7

Lessons in Love

Life as a police officer demanded everything from me—my time, my focus, my patience. Love, however, had its own way of slipping in when I wasn't looking. During this season, I dated casually. Nothing serious. Just moments, connections, lessons. Each woman revealed something to me—what I wanted, what I could tolerate, and what I absolutely could not. And there were more "could nots" than I expected.

Eventually, I stopped searching outward and turned inward. I poured my energy into school, working toward my bachelor's degree, convincing myself that ambition left no room for distraction. Love would have to wait.

Or so I thought.

One afternoon, while on patrol with my partner, Officer TW, we spotted someone she knew. We pulled over, exchanged greetings, and that's when I noticed him. He stood there casually in an orange T-shirt, dark blue jeans—unassuming, yet impossible to ignore. There was something about his presence. Clean. Grounded. Familiar.

Officer TW and he laughed easily, like people who shared history.

After a few minutes, he walked over and handed me his business card, smiling. "Call me if you need any work done on your house."

I smiled back, nodding politely. But inside, my thoughts were anything but polite. I'd seen him around before, just never noticed him. Until now.

The rest of that shift, his energy followed me. His voice. His smile. The way he smelled—subtle, warm, lingering. I hadn't felt that kind of pull in a long time.

"Girl," I said to Officer TW later, laughing, "he smells good." And his voice—damn, it got me excited.

She teased me without mercy, fully aware of my attraction to women. Then she got serious.

"Don't go there," she warned. "Don't start something you can't finish." "I know you," she said, laughing.

I gave her a look. No argument followed, but he stayed on my mind.

Over the next few days, I reached out. At first, we texted, though texting was never really his thing. Eventually, we talked. His voice was calm, steady, and strangely soothing.

I remember him inviting me to his place, and for whatever reason, I didn't go. I told him I had something to do, and that was that. At the time, it didn't feel like a big decision. Just one moment among many. But he never asked me over again.

Looking back now, I can't help but wonder what would have happened if I had gone. Would anything have been different? Or would we have ended up in the same place anyway, crossing paths again years later with the same unspoken tension and unanswered questions? Would he have taken my mind away?

I had loved women. Desired women. Craved women. That part of me was never in question. Yet The Artist stirred something unfamiliar, something that unsettled me. It wasn't just an attraction. It was recognition—the kind that bypasses logic and settles straight into the body. He reminded me of a girl I once loved from afar in high school, the kind of feeling that never quite leaves.

Every time he entered a room, my breath caught. Butterflies came back uninvited, and even now, they still do. He made me question parts of myself I thought were settled. We were never intimate, but the pull between us was undeniable. Dangerous, even. Not because of what happened, but because of what didn't.

We never dated. We respected each other. He knew where my heart usually lived, and I knew he would not cross certain lines. Still, we shared lunches, dinners, and long conversations that blurred boundaries in quiet ways. We took trips out of town together and stayed in the same hotel room, separate beds, but the energy in the room felt anything but separate. The quiet moments, the pauses between conversations, the awareness of each other's presence—those were the things that lingered.

Sometimes I wondered if he was testing my boundaries, or if I was testing my own. Neither of us said much. He would make little requests, like asking me to rub his shoulders, and I would laugh it off. The unspoken tension never needed a name, but it was there. I made sure he heard me when I returned to my space, and afterward, I promised myself not to take trips with him again unless separate rooms were part of the plan. The old me would have gotten exactly what she wanted.

The energy between us never fully went away. If anything, it became more noticeable in the silence, in the conversations that lasted a little too long, in the pauses that carried more than words. There was an understanding between us that never needed to be spoken aloud. Maybe that made it harder, because nothing had to happen for everything to be felt. We both knew what it was. We just chose not to name it.

As time went on, I had to be honest with myself about what this really was. It wasn't a relationship, and it wasn't growing into anything more. But it also wasn't nothing.

He understood how I felt without ever needing me to say it directly. Some things can be sensed without words. And I think he was intrigued by it. Not enough to act on it, just enough to leave it hanging in the air. That brought clarity; I didn't need validation. I didn't need explanations. I didn't need a different ending. What I needed was to stay grounded in myself.

The feelings did not disappear. I won't pretend they did. But I learned how to carry them differently—with less expectation and less attachment, and with more acceptance.

Still, The Artist lingered in thought and memory, in the spaces where possibility once lived.

I tried to move on. A few women tried to step into my world, but my heart wasn't available. It was elsewhere, caught between what felt right and what could never be.

That's when I understood the lesson.

Some connections should be ignored. Some people enter life not to stay, but to reveal what is unfinished inside us. The Artist was never meant to be my love story. He was my mirror.

And walking away did not mean I lost him. It meant I finally chose myself.

RETIREMENT AND REFLECTION

I finally retired from the police department after twenty years of service—twenty years of running toward danger, of holding people when life fell apart, of seeing the worst and the best of humanity. And just like that, I retired.

Leaving the badge behind was more than a change of schedule—it was stepping into a new life. The adrenaline, the sirens, the late-night calls, the heartbreaks—it all slowed down, and I had time to breathe, to think, to reflect.

For months, I revisited my life in my mind: childhood, teenage years, the first love, heartbreak, abuse, motherhood, rebuilding, police academy, patrol, and the friendships and loves that had shaped me. Each memory was a stitch in the quilt of who I had become.

And yet, some wounds remained open. My mother's death in 2022 left a strange emptiness.

Our complicated relationship had never allowed me peace, and now, without her presence, I had to confront all the lingering questions and anger I had buried for years. Forgiveness didn't come immediately—it came slowly, like a tide. I realized I didn't need her validation anymore, only an understanding of myself.

Hoops, JB, The Artist, my children, the women I had loved, even the fleeting connections—they all reminded me of the paths I had walked. Each one was a lesson, a challenge, a gift. The memory of The Artist was still sharp, thrilling, and dangerous in the quiet moments. The pull, the curiosity, the questioning of my identity—it was still there, simmering.

Retirement gave me time to honor all of it. Time to sit with grief, love, desire, and identity without interruption. I could finally reflect on who I was, who I had been, and who I wanted to become.

I realized life isn't about perfection. It's about endurance, choices, and being present. The badge may be gone, but the lessons, the scars, and the triumphs stayed with me. They were mine to carry, mine to learn from, mine to cherish.

It was a new beginning. A chance to focus on myself, my family, and the connections that truly mattered. The quiet, reflective moments showed me that love exists in forms beyond the obvious—sometimes dangerous, sometimes platonic, sometimes quiet, sometimes exhilarating. And sometimes, it exists just to remind you that your heart is still alive.

CHAPTER 9

LIFE AFTER RETIREMENT

Starting a new chapter was more than leaving the badge behind—it was stepping into a world that I had longed to see from the other side. After twenty years of running toward emergencies, heartache, and the chaos of life, I finally had time to breathe, to heal, to reflect, and to explore the parts of myself I had set aside.

The early days were quiet—too quiet at times. The adrenaline I had grown accustomed to was gone. No sirens, no urgent calls, no lives hanging in the balance on my watch. And yet, the lessons of policing stayed with me: discipline, empathy, patience, courage. They weren't just tools for the job—they became a part of how I moved through life.

Time gave me space to reconnect. Old friends, long-lost connections, the people I had loved and lost—all of them became part of the reflection. My children thrived in the rhythm of stability. I found joy in watching them grow; in knowing I could be present without the constant pull of duty.

I revisited old passions, those I had abandoned during the years: painting, writing, exploring creativity that had long been dormant. Each stroke, each word, reminded me of a self I had almost forgotten. These hobbies weren't just pastimes—they were acts of reclaiming identity.

And the memories... The Artist, Hoops, JB, Old Man—each name, a story, a heartbeat of my life. The Artist still lingered in quiet moments, in stolen thoughts, in the hum of possibility that never fully went away. JB remained my steady friend, our bond deepened by years of shared growth and understanding. My high school crush, Hoops, remained a touchstone of first love and raw discovery, a reminder of what had always shaped my heart.

Through reflection, I realized that life is a series of intersections. Some people walk in and out of your story, leaving only lessons. Others stay, changing the trajectory of everything. And some, like Swift or JB, challenge you to see yourself more clearly than you ever could alone.

I understood that my life—every heartbreak, every joy, every loss, every triumph—was a collage of experiences. Retirement wasn't an endpoint. It was a vantage point, a place to observe the patterns, to honor the struggles, and to choose which threads I wanted to weave into the next chapter of life.

Most importantly, I discovered my resilience. I am capable of joy, desire, reflection, and growth. Retirement didn't remove the weight of the past, but it gave me the clarity to carry it with wisdom. Life after service became a conscious choice: to live with intention, to love without fear, and to embrace every moment as my own.

CHAPTER 10

LOOKING FORWARD

Time to breathe, to reflect, and most importantly, time to look forward instead of constantly reacting to the past.

I realized that my journey—from childhood to high school, through heartbreak, motherhood, and years on the force—had shaped me into someone who could finally take ownership of her life. Every experience, painful or joyful, had taught me lessons in resilience, love, and identity.

Looking forward wasn't about escaping the past. It was about honoring it. I could finally see the way every choice, every heartbreak, every triumph had guided me here, to a place of understanding and clarity.

I thought about my children, my high school crush Hoops, JB, and The Artist—the people who had left indelible marks on my heart. They were reminders that life's beauty often comes from its complexity. Some doors close, yes, but others open in ways you never could have predicted.

Now, my focus was on legacy and purpose. I wanted to leave behind something meaningful, not just for my children, but for anyone who might look at my life and see proof that survival, resilience, and self-love are possible. My story could show that love comes in many forms—not always conventional, not always easy—but always worth honoring.

I also recognized the importance of curiosity and exploration. Retirement didn't mean stagnation; it meant freedom. Freedom to pursue passions, to try new things, to rediscover the parts of myself I had left behind in the chaos of life. Writing, painting, volunteering, building deeper connections—these weren't just hobbies—they were acts of reclamation.

Looking forward means choosing joy even when shadows linger. It means embracing desire, love, and curiosity without guilt. It means setting boundaries, respecting my needs, and understanding that my happiness was my responsibility—not anyone else's.

As I stepped into this next chapter, I felt a quiet excitement, a steady confidence. Life was still unpredictable, still messy, but now I could face it on my terms. The lessons of the past were mine to carry, not to weigh me down. The future is mine to shape, moment by moment, decision by decision.

Looking forward isn't just hope—it's intentional living. It's choosing to honor my story, my desires, and my heart. It's the beginning of a life fully claimed, fully embraced, and fully alive.

CHAPTER 11

REDISCOVERING DESIRE

After years of focusing on survival, responsibility, and rebuilding, I realized something: desire doesn't fade—it waits. Patient, insistent, daring you to notice it. And notice it I did.

I had spent so much time protecting my heart, shielding my emotions, prioritizing my children, my career, my growth. But now, in the quiet spaces of retirement, I felt it stir again—the pull of curiosity, attraction, and even the dangerous thrill of the unknown.

I explored connections with women casually, as I had in my younger years, but now it felt different. There was depth, intention, and playfulness. I noticed the way glances lingered, the way touch sparked thought, the thrill of emotional intimacy without expectation. Desire had evolved—it was sharper, richer, and more nuanced.

And then there was The Artist.

Even years later, he lingered like a ghost I welcomed. Every conversation, every laugh, every subtle touch reminded me that some connections leave permanent marks. Desire with him wasn't just physical—it was emotional, intellectual, spiritual. He made me question boundaries, identity, and the very definitions I had held about myself.

Yet, there was safety in it, too. I felt protected around him. My vulnerabilities didn't feel like weaknesses—they felt like trust. In his presence, I could explore parts of myself I had long denied, quietly, without shame. It was intoxicating, this dance of desire without possession.

And it wasn't just The Artist. New connections appeared in unexpected ways, people who challenged my perceptions of intimacy, identity, and love. Some were platonic, some flirtatious, some pushed my limits emotionally. Each relationship mirrored something I needed to see in myself—my capacity to desire, to feel, to love, to question, to grow.

Desire became a teacher. It reminded me that attraction isn't just physical, that love isn't always defined by convention, and that boundaries are not limits—they're protections that allow exploration to feel safe.

Through these experiences, I learned to honor my urges without shame, to explore emotional and physical intimacy with honesty, and to recognize the rare and electric moments that stir the heart in ways both thrilling and terrifying.

Rediscovering desire wasn't reckless. It was reclaiming parts of myself I had tucked away for survival. It was breathing in life fully—lust, longing, laughter, and love. And in that reclamation, I realized: I am whole. I am alive. I am unapologetically me.

CHAPTER 12

UNEXPECTED CONNECTIONS

Life has a way of surprising you when you least expect it. Just when I thought I had mapped out my world—my boundaries, my desires, my identity—new connections appeared, knocking over every assumption. Some were subtle at first. A smile that lingered too long. A conversation that sparked curiosity. A friend who seemed to understand me without explanation. They weren't always romantic, but they pushed me to see myself differently.

I found platonic relationships could be just as intoxicating as romantic ones. People who challenged me, mirrored my thoughts, or simply held space for my truth reminded me that intimacy isn't always physical. There's a hunger for understanding, for safety, for being seen—and sometimes, that hunger is more powerful than lust.

And then there was The Artist again—ever-present in memory and in quiet touches of reality. His friendship was complicated, electric, protective, and safe all at once. I never stopped questioning my attraction, identity, and my desires around him. Every glance, every laugh, every subtle shift in his energy reminded me that boundaries could be thrilling, even when nothing physical passed between us.

Unexpectedly, new women entered my life, each offering something different: laughter, honesty, teasing challenges. Some forced me to confront parts of myself I had ignored—my fears, my cravings, my longings. Some mirrored the old me, daring and reckless. Others reflected the wiser me, more cautious, but still hungry.

Through it all, I realized that connections—expected or unexpected—were mirrors. They forced me to examine my desires, my limits, and my capacity to love without losing myself.

I learned to embrace these moments fully, even when they scared me. Each connection became a lesson: trust yourself, honor your needs, respect boundaries, and allow the heart to feel freely without guilt.

Unexpected connections reminded me that life doesn't always follow plans. Desire, intimacy, and love show up in strange, complicated, sometimes dangerous ways. And sometimes, the people who challenge you most are the ones who shape you deepest.

I learned to lean into the discomfort, to savor the thrill, and to allow myself to feel fully—because the magic in life often exists in the unexpected.

CHAPTER 13

THE ARTIST RETURNS

Just when I thought the currents of my life had settled, he reappeared. The man who had stirred something dangerous and irresistible inside me years ago. And suddenly, the quiet stability I'd built felt like sand slipping through my fingers. We ran into each other at a coffee shop. I hadn't expected to see him. And yet, there he was—effortless, magnetic, the same energy I remembered, intensified. That smile, that laugh, the subtle way he noticed me before anyone else in the room. My chest tightened. My pulse sped up. Butterflies exploded like fireworks in my stomach.

He greeted me as if no time had passed, but the years had changed us both. His eyes held something new—depth, reflection, a quiet knowing. And yet, beneath it all, that same spark lingered, dangerous and thrilling.

We spent hours talking that night. Not about work, not about life plans, not about boundaries—just us, in a room that felt both intimate and vast. Every word, every glance, every pause mirrored something inside me I hadn't dared confront for years. Desire, curiosity, longing—all tangled together in a raw, unspoken way.

There was a protective energy in him, too. Subtle gestures—standing closer when the crowd pressed in, listening intently when I spoke, a hand lightly brushing mine to guide me through the shop. It wasn't possessive; it wasn't aggressive—it was steady, grounded, safe. And yet, it inflamed the parts of me I thought I had controlled.

The conversation ended, but the tension didn't. We left the coffee shop separately, yet neither of us truly left the other behind. That night, I lay awake thinking about him—the warmth, the pull, the danger of a connection so intense and undefined. It reminded me of my younger self, the Hoops-era heart, wild and daring. And yet, it was tempered by years of knowing, of boundaries, of survival.

The Artist's return forced me to confront truths I had tucked away. Desire isn't always about action—it can be about recognition, curiosity, and the thrill of being seen by someone who gets you. Our connection was complicated. It was emotional, physical, spiritual—and it defied definition.

I had to remind myself: boundaries are not limitations—they're protection. But protection doesn't mean denying yourself the rush, the pull, the excitement of being truly alive.

And so, I allowed myself to feel. Deeply. Fully. Recklessly, in the quiet corners of my mind and the subtle moments of presence with him. Because some love, some desire, some connection—you can't cage it. You can only honor it, navigate it, and let it teach you who you are and what you are capable of feeling.

The Artist had returned, and with him came a mirror: of desire, of identity, of courage. And I realized something crucial—sometimes, the people who challenge you most are the ones who remind you that your heart is still alive, still capable, still dangerous in the best way possible.

CHAPTER 14

THE DEPTH OF FRIENDSHIP

Not all love is romantic. Some of the most powerful connections in life are friendships that hold you steady when the world feels like it's falling apart. After The Artist's return, I realized just how much I had leaned on platonic love over the years. JB, Hoops, my close colleagues—they weren't just people I spent time with—they were mirrors, protectors, challengers, and confidants all at once.

Friendship had a quiet kind of intimacy. No expectations beyond presence. No pressure beyond honesty. Yet, somehow, it demanded more of me than many romantic relationships ever had. It asked for authenticity, for patience, for trust.

Officer TW remained my sounding board, my partner in chaos, the person who could read between my words and understand the subtext of my silences. Her teasing, her laughter, and her loyalty reminded me that love is not always about passion—it can be about safety.

JB, the one who had shared years of my life, still provided a steadying presence even after our romantic connection had evolved into a platonic one. She saw my pain, my growth, my mistakes, and she stayed—not out of obligation, but because she valued me, my truth, and my journey. She loved me through the pain.

The Artist, however, his presence complicated everything. His friendship and desire, boundaries and temptation, protection and fire.

With him, I felt seen in a way I hadn't with anyone else. And that recognition, that intensity, reminded me that some of the deepest connections aren't easy—they are layered, messy, and transformative.

Finally, I understood that platonic love could teach you as much about yourself as romantic love. It could challenge you, heal you, and remind you of your worth. It could hold you accountable without judgment, encourage growth without manipulation, and provide a safe space to explore desires, fears, and identity.

Through friendship, I learned the importance of loyalty, honesty, and presence. I discovered that emotional intimacy isn't about labels—it's about the willingness to show up for someone, to listen, and to honor the connection.

These friendships became anchors in my life. They reminded me that love is multifaceted. It exists in laughter, in quiet moments, in the way someone notices your smallest gestures and still stays.

And through it all, I realized the depth of friendship isn't just about surviving together—it's about thriving together, and allowing each other to become the fullest, truest versions of yourselves. In the end, friendship proved that love, in any form, has the power to heal, transform, and ignite.

CHAPTER 15

LOVE REIMAGINED

Love had always been a teacher—sometimes gentle, sometimes brutal—but it had never been simple. Now, years later, I found myself standing at the intersection of past and present, desire and restraint, curiosity and caution.

The Artist remained a presence in my life, not defined by labels, not bound by expectation, but electric in every interaction. His return reminded me that love isn't always neat or conventional. It could be messy, complicated, emotionally raw, and still transformative.

I allowed myself to explore that complexity. The pull between us was undeniable—charged with longing, with memory, with the thrill of being truly seen. And yet, there were boundaries. Mutual respect. Unspoken rules that kept us safe while igniting the fire between us. Desire didn't always need to be acted upon to exist; sometimes, it was enough to feel it, to let it shape you.

JB, Old Man, and the woman who entered my life also showed me a different side of love. Friendship, loyalty, teasing, challenges, laughter, protection, and emotional depth—they all contributed to my understanding of what it meant to connect. Love could be platonic, romantic, or something entirely new—fluid, developing, alive.

Through it all, I realized that love was not a destination—it was a practice. A choice. A series of moments where honesty, respect, and presence mattered more than passion alone. I reimagined what it meant to love: fiercely, intentionally, and without apology.

There were nights when desire and longing collided, when the weight of unspoken attraction made my chest tighten, my pulse race. And there were quiet moments, too—shared smiles, knowing glances, laughter that carried unspoken understanding. Both were **love**. Both were valid. Both were transformative.

I finally understood that love doesn't always follow the rules you expect. It doesn't arrive neatly packaged. It challenges you, questions you, ignites you, and sometimes leaves you breathless with longing. But when you honor it—fully, honestly, and without fear—it teaches you the deepest lessons of self-awareness, trust, and courage.

Love reimagined wasn't about perfection. It wasn't about owning or possessing. It was about presence, connection, and the willingness to show up fully, for yourself and for those who mattered. In this new understanding, I felt freer than I had ever felt before—alive, whole, and ready to embrace whatever form love chose to take.

CHAPTER 16

FULL CIRCLE

Life has a way of coming back around, of returning to the truths we once thought we left behind. Standing at this point in my journey, I could see the patterns—the heartbreak, the lessons, the loves, the losses—and I understood them for the first time.

I thought about my children, my first love, Hoops, Old Man, The Artist, and all the fleeting connections that had shaped me. Each one had left a mark, a lesson, a reflection of who I was and who I could become.

But now, I approached that energy with awareness, with boundaries, with gratitude. The fire between us was thrilling, but I no longer feared it or tried to suppress it. I could feel it, honor it, and let it exist without consuming me.

My friendships—JB, Old Man, Hoops, my chosen family—remained anchors, reminders that love comes in many forms and that safety, trust, and honesty are as vital as desire and passion. Platonic bonds had taught me resilience, patience, and the quiet power of being seen without judgment.

I also recognized the journey of self-love. Every heartbreak, every betrayal, every loss had pushed me toward this place of authenticity. I finally understood that love—romantic, platonic, familial, or even the unspoken pull of desire— always starts with oneself. The clearer I became about my worth, the richer every connection felt.

Looking back, I saw the little Hoops who once snuck around with me, terrified of judgment, desperate for acceptance. I saw the mother navigating trauma and loss. I saw the officer balancing empathy and authority. And I saw the woman who had reclaimed herself again and again, refusing to be defined by anyone else's narrative.

Coming full circle wasn't about erasing the past—it was about embracing it. About seeing every trial, every joy, every loss as a thread in the fabric of my life. And in doing so, I found peace. A fierce, unshakable peace.

Life is messy. It's beautiful. It's cruel and tender in the same breath. But in the end, it taught me one undeniable truth: to live fully, to love fully, and to honor every part of yourself along the way.

I am whole. I am alive. I am unapologetically me.

And as I look forward, I know this: the story isn't over. It's just entering a new chapter. One written not by the chaos of the past, but by the wisdom, courage, and love I carry into every tomorrow.

EPILOGUE

LEARNING TO LOVE YOURSELF

Looking back, every heartbreak, triumph, and lesson led to one truth: you must learn to love yourself first.

Love yourself fiercely, honor your journey, embrace your identity, and give without losing yourself.

Life is a journey, and it begins with you.